NEW METHOD

FOR REPRESENTING BY DOTS THE FORM OF LETTERS

MAPS, GEOMETRIC FIGURES SYMBOLS OF MUSIC, ETC.

FOR USE BY THE BLIND

LOUIS BRAILLE

Tutor at the Royal Institution of Young Blinds of Paris

*

1839

Éditions Nielrow

Dijon – France - 2018

ISBN : 978-2-490446-06-3

THE 1839 BROCHURE

TRANSLATED BY IMPLEX

CONTENTS

The original text of Louis Braille had never been reissued since 1839 until 2016 ; it was then reissued in French, by Éditions Nielrow. This is the translation of the original text that is reproduce here.

To get blind people to write, to make them overcome this obstacle, which restricts so considerably their social relations, is a challenge tempted by all those who have occupied themselves with their education ; it is a subject that should have been proposed for price by the various improvement schools ; perhaps one will find that I've contributed to bringing solution to that problem.

Sometimes, we see blind people writing with more or less complicated apparatus ; but these are only rare exceptions which attest the power of skill united to intelligence, without constituting a general and easy method of writing. Moreover, these privileged blinds cannot read their writings, nor even be certain that their pencil or black paper has been marked enough : a lot of considerations to disastrous consequences and pitfalls that I proposed to avoid, by a process which success is strongly due to Mr. Fournier, worthy pupil and great collaborator of Valentin Haüy, the founder of the first institutions for the education of the blind, in France and in Russia.

To mark on the paper dots that represent the form of the letters and to make reliefs on it, that is the whole purpose of this new method of writing. M. Barbier has imagined representing sounds and articulations by group of dots based on very ingenious combinations ; he then allowed me to modify his process, by reducing the number of dots of each group, which provides a new writing method very widespread today among the blind : "But, it was said, that these are only conventions, and only the initiates can read the written pages according to these two methods." Although these objections are unfounded since a few lines of explanation are enough to make these two methods fully known, they have nevertheless been the cause of new research which has led me to a process of which here is the explanation.

To form the letters, I have observed that if we put four dots on the body of each character, we'll need three dots for the upper tail and three dots for the lower tail as well, which produces for the whole height of the letter, a vertical height of ten dots marked or not, depending on whether the character requires it or not. We also can only give three dots of height to the body of the letter and only two dots to each tail, which provides a finer writing, but less regular than the other. Each letter is thus formed of a series of vertical lines : letter B, for example, is represented by four lines ; in the first are marked the 1st, the 2nd, the 3rd, the 4th, the 5th and the 6th dot; in the second, 4th and 7th; in the third, the 3rd and the 7th; in the fourth, the 5th and the 6th.

We would analyze in the same way, the other letters and the most irregular forms that one can imagine; by extension, geographic maps, geometric figures, and the whole musical system.

The capital letter M, so remarkable for its size, is formed of twelve vertical lines, each composed of dots whose position is marked by the following numbers :

1st line 1,7

2nd line 1,2,3,4,5,6,7

3th line 2,3,7

4th line 3,4

5th line 4,5

6th line 6,7

7th line 5

8th line 4

9th line 3,7

10th line 1,2,3,4,5,6,7

11th line 1,2,3,4,5,6,7

12th line 1,7

In order to write, we have planks of wood or metal, on which are drawn tracts each formed often concave and horizontal lines ; a sort of wire is applied to each litter, the days of which are high enough to let the ten rays be seen, and are wide enough to make two dots head on of each line.

The paper is placed between the board and the wire, and with the help of a simple dot the letters are made, marking for this purpose, the dots indicated by the ciphered table of the form of the letters, or by the spirit individual, observing : 1° that the

letters from right to left must be written :
2° to overthrow each letter so that the first
line on the left, when reading, is the first on
the right when writing. This way of writing
is facilitated by applying on the mesh one or
more extremely thin crosspieces, to make
better known the position of the tails and the
body of the letter. I will observe that we will
at the same time obtain several copies of
what we write, placing one on the other as
many sheets as we want copies and marking
the dots on the whole.

The striped board may be replaced by a
board covered with leather, fleece or any
other object that produces a slight crease ;
the mesh may be a wire mesh, a punched
plate punch, or a meeting of cross-threads at
right angles and welded to one another.

For the foregoing, it is known that any
blind person, possessing the small apparatus
described above and the ciphered chart can,
without any teacher and in a few days only,
learn to write, even though he would be
devoid of skill and remarkable intelligence.

The Institution of the Blind Young of Paris has just melted types representing a vertical often sensitive or non-sensitive dots ; several of these characters, combined with each other, give the form of the letter on large dimensions ; this allows the blind to easily analyze each letter and reproduce it on paper using his writing board. Alphabets are printed with the types, which are attached to the numbered table, so that each person can learn to form the letter, either by inspection or by knowing the numbers representing the dots to score.

The device to highlight geometric figures and geographic maps etc. consists of a frame on which rests a moving ruler ; on this ruler are drawn vertical lines of half a line-wide and distant from each other of the same dimension. This device is applied to the card that we want to reproduce, and we place the ruler at the top of the frame ; we examine what are the territorial limits, the mountains, the rivers, etc., which lead to the rays of the ruler, and one write on a notebook the figures indicating these rays.

Then we go down half-line rule, we do the same examination as before, and we go on the same way until the card is fully ciphered.

The map is reproduced by marking dots on the paper, whose place is indicated by the ciphered catalog ; the moving ruler or fences, explained above, will guide to find the position of the dots.

To write music, you must :

1° Have a board covered with leather, both overcome by a frame ;

2° Mark on the leather the spans formed, each of the eleven parallel and concave lines ; the lines must be far enough apart one from another so that, four dots can be placed between two adjacent ones ;

3° Put the paper between the leather and the chassis, and give it the imprint of the leather's lines, making sure to cut the first three and the last three lines of each range : these lines will be used as the small lines used in ordinary music, and they will be well noticed from the five continuous lines which represent the outline ;

4° Place on each span a grid in the days of which we can mark the dots representing the shape of the music characters, for which we can also have a ciphered catalog.

M. Binet, a distinguished pupil from the Institution of Paris, has conceived jointly with me, several years ago, a method of writing simpler than the preceding one, but less advantageous in its results. To write according to this system, it is necessary 1° Have a board on which is applied a leather ; 2° Cover the board with a frame on which are fixed horizontal crosspieces wide enough to receive the eye of the letter which must be marked there ; 3° Possess a small locker that can contain two letters of each kind, which must be of metal, so it can, favorably, be formed by a series of dots.

To write thanks to this apparatus, we take the letters that we need out of the locker one after another, then we push them on the paper between the board and the frame, and then we carefully put back the letters that were used in the locker. Although in practice this mode of writing is imperfect, I have indicated it, because it will perhaps be preferred by non-blinds who, without preparatory exercise, will want to write to the blind and be read by them ; however, I am confident that they will use the other method more successfully.

Several attempts have been made, more or less fortunate, to blacken our new writing : for example, we can place a blackened paper under the sheet on which we wish to write, according to the methods used commercially ; but the white sheet touching the black sheet by shock and not by friction, is only faintly colored by it. Without a doubt, one day, art and experience will help discover a chemical composition that will remove these disadvantages.

***

TABLE OF THE FORM OF THE LETTERS

a.   5 6 | 4 7 | 4 7 | 3 4 5 6 | 7.

b.   1 2 3 4 5 6 | 4 7 | 4 7 | 5 6.

c.   5 6 | 4 7 | 4 7.

d.   5 6 | 1 4 7 | 1 4 7 | 2 3 4 5 6.

e.   5 6 | 4 5 7 | 4 5 7.

f.   9 | 10 | 2 3 4 5 6 7 8 9 | 1 4 | 2.

g.   5 6 | 4 7 10 | 4 7 10 | 3 4 5 6 7 8 9.

h.   1 2 3 4 5 6 7 | 4 | 4 5 6 7 | 7.

i.   2 4 5 6 7 | 7.

j.   9 | 10 | 2 4 5 6 7 8 9.

k.   1 2 3 4 5 6 7 | 5 6 | 4 7.

l.   1 2 3 4 5 6 7 | 7.

m.   4 5 6 7 | 4 | 4 5 6 7 | 4 | 4 5 6 7 | 7.

n.   4 5 6 7 | 4 | 4 5 6 7 | 7.

o.   5 6 | 4 7 | 4 7 | 5 6.

p.   3 4 5 6 7 8 9 10 | 4 7 | 4 7 | 5 6.

q.   5 6 | 4 7 | 4 7 | 3 4 5 6 7 8 9 10.

r.   4 5 6 7 | 4 | 4.

s.   6 | 7 | 4 5 6 | 3.

t.   2 3 4 5 6 7 | 4 7.

u.   4 5 6 7 | 7 | 4 5 6 7 | 7.

v.   4 5 | 6 7 | 6 | 4 5.

w.   4 5 | 6 7 | 6 | 4 5 | 6 7 | 6 | 4 5.

x.   4 7 | 4 7 | 5 6 | 4 7 | 4 7.

y.   4 | 4 5 6 7 10 | 7 10 | 4 5 6 7 8
9.

z.   4 7 | 4 6 7 | 4 5 7 | 4 7.

ç.   5 6 | 4 7 10 | 4 7 9.

ae.   5 6 | 4 7 | 4 7 | 3 4 5 6 | 4 5 7 | 4
5 7.

oe.   5 6 | 4 7 | 4 7 | 5 6 | 4 5 7 | 4 5
7.

é.   5 6 | 2 4 5 7 | 1 4 5 7.

à.   5 6 | 1 4 7 | 2 4 7 | 4 5 6 | 7.

è.   5 6 | 1 4 5 7 | 2 4 5 7.

ì.   1 | 2 4 5 6 7 | 7.

ò.   5 6 | 1 4 7 | 2 4 7 | 5 6.

ù.   4 5 6 7 | 1 7 | 2 4 5 6 7 | 7.

â.   5 6 | 2 4 7 | 1 4 7 | 2 4 5 6 | 7.

ê.   2 5 6 | 1 4 5 7 | 2 4 5 7.

î.   2 | 1 4 5 6 7 | 2 7.

ô.   5 6 | 2 4 7 | 1 4 7 | 2 5 6.

û.   2 4 5 6 7 | 1 7 | 2 4 5 6 7 | 7.

ë.   5 6 | 2 4 5 7 | 2 4 5 7.

ï.   2 4 5 6 7 | 2 7.

ü.   4 5 6 7 | 2 7 | 2 4 5 6 7 | 7.

A.   7 | 6 7 | 5 7 | 4 5 | 3 5 | 2 5 7 | 1
2 3 4 5 6 7 | 1 2 3 4 5 6 7 | 7.

B.   1 7 | 1 2 3 4 5 6 7 | 1 2 3 4 5 6 7
| 1 4 7 | 1 4 7 | 1 2 3 4 5 6 7 | 2 3 5 6.

C.   3 4 5 | 2 3 4 5 6 | 1 7 | 1 7 | 1 7 |
2 6.

D.   1 7 | 1 2 3 4 5 6 7 | 1 2 3 4 2 6 7
(sic) | 1 7 | 1 7 | 2 3 4 5 6 | 3 4 5.

E.   1 7 | 1 2 3 4 5 6 7 | 1 2 3 4 5 6 7
| 1 4 7 | 1 3 4 5 7 | 1 7 | 1 2 6 7.

F.   1 7 | 1 2 3 4 5 6 7 | 1 2 3 4 5 6 7
| 1 4 7 | 1 3 4 5 | 1 | 1 2.

G.   3 4 5 | 2 3 4 5 6 | 1 7 | 1 5 7 | 1
5 6 7 | 2 5 6 | 5.

H.   1 7 | 1 2 3 4 5 6 7 | 1 2 3 4 5 6 7 | 1 4 7 | 4 | 1 4 7 | 1 2 3 4 5 6 7 | 1 2 3 4 5 6 7 | 1 7.

I.   1 7 | 1 2 3 4 5 6 7 | 1 2 3 4 5 6 | 1 7.

J.   6 7 | 1 7 | 1 2 3 4 5 6 7 | 1 2 3 4 5 6 | 1.

K.   1 7 | 1 2 3 4 5 6 7 | 1 2 3 4 5 6 7 | 1 4 7 | 3 5 | 1 2 6 7 | 1 7.

L.   1 7 | 1 2 3 4 5 6 7 | 1 2 3 4 5 6 7 | 1 7 | 7 | 7 | 6 7.

M.   1 7 | 1 2 3 4 5 6 7 | 2 3 7 | 3 4 | 4 5 | 6 7 | 5 | 4 | 3 7 | 1 2 3 4 5 6 7 | 1 2 3 4 5 6 7 | 1 7.

N.   1 7 | 1 2 3 4 5 6 7 | 1 2 7 | 2 3 | 3 4 | 4 5 | 5 6 | 1 6 7 | 1 2 3 4 5 6 7 | 4.

O.   3 4 5 | 2 3 4 5 6 | 1 7 | 1 7 | 1 7 | 2 3 4 5 6 | 3 4 5.

P.   1 7 | 1 2 3 4 5 6 7 | 1 2 3 4 5 6 7 | 1 4 7 | 1 4 | 1 2 3 4 | 2 3.

Q.   3 4 5 | 2 3 4 5 6 | 1 7 | 1 7 8 | 1 7 9 | 2 3 4 5 6 10 | 3 4 5.

R.   1 7 | 1 2 3 4 5 6 7 | 1 2 3 4 5 6 7 | 1 4 7 | 1 4 | 1 2 3 4 5 6 | 2 3 5 6 7 | 7.

S.   6 | 7 | 7 | 2 3 4 5 6 7 | 1 2 3 4 5 6 | 1 | 1 | 2.

T.   1 2 | 1 | 1 7 | 1 2 3 4 5 6 7 | 1 2 3 4 5 6 7 | 1 7 | 1 | 1 2.

U.   1 | 1 2 3 4 5 6 | 1 2 3 4 5 6 7 | 1 7 | 7 | 1 7 | 1 2 3 4 5 6 | 1.

V.   1 | 1 2 3 4 5 6 7 | 1 2 3 4 5 6 7 | 1 6 | 5 | 4 | 1 3 | 1 2 | 1.

W.   1 | 1 2 3 4 5 6 7 | 1 2 3 4 5 6 7 | 1 6 | 5 | 4 | 1 3 | 1 2 3 4 5 6 7 | 1 2 3 4 5 6 7 | 1 6 | 5 | 4 | 1 3 | 1 2 | 1.

X.   1 7 | 1 2 6 7 | 1 2 3 5 7 | 1 3 4 | 4 5 7 | 1 2 5 6 7 | 1 2 6 7 | 1 7.

Y.   1 | 1 2 | 1 2 3 7 | 1 3 4 5 6 7 | 4 5 6 7 | 1 3 7 | 1 2 | 1.

Z.   1 2 6 7 | 1 5 6 7 | 1 4 5 7 | 1 3 4

7 | 1 2 3 7 | 1 2 6 7.

Ç.   3 4 5 | 2 3 4 5 6 | 1 7 10 | 1 7 9 | 1 7 | 2 6.

AE.   7 | 6 7 | 5 7 | 4 5 | 3 5 | 2 5 7 | 1 2 3 4 5 6 7 | 1 2 3 4 5 6 7 | 1 4 7 | 1 3 4 5 7 | 1 7 | 1 2 6 7.

OE.   3 4 5 | 2 3 4 5 6 | 1 7 | 1 7 | 1 7 | 2 6 | 1 2 3 4 5 6 7 | 1 2 3 4 5 6 7 | 1 4 7 | 1 3 4 5 7 | 1 7 | 1 2 6 7.

FIGURES

1.   3 7 | 3 4 5 6 7 | 3 7.

2.   3 7 | 2 6 7 | 2 5 7 | 3 4 7.

3.   2 6 | 1 7 | 1 4 7 | 2 3 5 6.

4.   6 | 5 6 | 4 6 | 3 6 | 2 4 5 6 7 | 1 6.

5.   3 4 6 | 2 4 7 | 1 4 7 | 1 5 6.

6.   4 5 6 | 3 7 | 2 4 7 | 1 5 6.

7.   10 | 9 | 4 8 | 4 7 | 4 6 | 4 5 | 4.

8.   2 3 5 6 | 1 4 7 | 1 4 7 | 2 3 5 6.

9.   5 6 10 | 4 7 9 | 4 8 | 5 6 7.

0.   5 6 | 4 7 | 4 7 | 5 6.

PONCTUATION AND OTHER SIGNS

.   7.

:   5 7.

,   8 | 7

;   8 | 5 7.

?   1 3 4 5 7 | 2.

!   1 2 3 4 5 7.

-       6 | 6 | 6.

'   2 | 9.

(4 5 6 7 | 3 8 | 2 9 | 1 10.

)   1 10 | 2 9 | 3 8 | 4 5 6 7.

*   3 5 | 4 | 1 4 7 | 2 3 4 5 6 | 1 4 7 | 4 | 3 5.

«   5 6 | 4 5 6 7 | 4 7.

»   4 7 | 4 5 6 7 | 5 6.

Finis

***

PRINTING OF MADAME HUZARD
(BORN VALLAT CHAPEL)
Rue de l'Eperon, n ° 7

Nielrow Editions
frwor@outlook.com

Louis Braille : *Nouveau procédé pour représenter...*
Charles Suisse : *Restauration du château de Dijon*
Victor Coissac : *La conquête de l'espace*
J.O.B. : *Les épées de France*
Casimir Coquilhat : *Trajectoires des fusées volantes*
Implex : *Mots croisés ; 49 défis*
Arnold Netter : *De l'argent colloïdal*
Robert de Launay : *La question des effectifs à Alésia*
Jean-Baptiste Savigny : *Radeau de la Méduse*
Beaumarchais : *Essai sur le genre dramatique*
Pierre Louis de Maupertuis : *Voyage en Laponie*
Dr Wiart : *De l'usage interne de l'eau de mer*
Corneille de Nélis : *La pierre Brunehaut*
Abbé Mann : *Dissertation sur les déluges*
John Law : *The company of Mississipi (english/french)*
Louis Braille : *New method for representing...*

Legal deposit at BNF
Nielrow Editions
4rd quarter 2018

www.ingramcontent.com/pod-product-compliance
Lightning Source LLC
Chambersburg PA
CBHW030012040426
42337CB00012BA/746